D1547670

*The Aquinas Lecture, 1977*

# THE PROBLEM OF EVIL

Under the auspices of the
Wisconsin-Alpha Chapter of Phi Sigma Tau

By
ERROL E. HARRIS, D.Litt.

MARQUETTE UNIVERSITY PUBLICATIONS
MILWAUKEE
1977

Library of Congress Catalog Card Number 77-72325

# Prefatory

The Wisconsin Alpha Chapter of Phi Sigma Tau, the National Honor Society for Philosophy at Marquette University, each year invites a scholar to lecture in honor of St. Thomas Aquinas. This year the lecture was delivered on Sunday, February 27.

The 1977 Aquinas Lecture, *The Problem of Evil*, was delivered in Todd Wehr Chemistry by Professor Errol E. Harris, Distinguished Visiting Professor of Philosophy, Marquette University.

Professor Harris was born February 19, 1908 in Kimberley, South Africa. He earned the B.A. in 1927 and the M.A. in 1929 at Rhodes University College, Grahamstown, South Africa. In 1933 he earned the B.Litt. at Magdalen College, Oxford, and in 1951 the D.Litt. at the University of Witwatersrand, Johannesburg, S.A. He began teaching at Fort Hare University College in 1930 and then from 1937 to 1942 he was education officer in the British Colonial Service in Basutoland and Zanzibar. During World War II he served first in the

South African Information Service and then in the British Army Educational Corps. After the war he returned to South Africa and taught at the University of Witwatersrand. In 1953 he was made head of the department of philosophy in that university. Professor Harris came to the United States in 1956 and served as Visiting Professor at Yale University and then as Professor at Connecticut College until 1962, except for the year 1959-1960 when he was acting head of the Department of Logic and Metaphysics at Univeristy of Edinburgh, Scotland. From 1962 to 1966 he was Roy Roberts Distinguished Professor at the University of Kansas and in 1966 Professor of Philosophy at Northwestern University; he became the John Evans Professor of Moral and Intellectual Philosophy in 1974. Professor Harris is Distinguished Visiting Professor of Philosophy at Marquette University in the current year.

Professor Harris was the Terry Lecturer (Yale, 1957), the Heinz Werner Lecturer (Clark, 1973) and the Machette Lecturer (Tulane, 1975). He served as president of the Metaphysical Society of America in 1968-69.

Professor Harris' study and interest range over the philosophy of science, the theory of knowledge, political philosophy, metaphysics, and the history of modern philosophy. Among his numerous publications are: *The Survival of Political Man* (1950); *Nature, Mind and Modern Science* (1954); *Revelation through Reason* (1958); *The Foundations of Metaphysics in Science* (1965); *Annihilation and Utopia* (1966); *Hypothesis and Perception* (1970); *Salvation from Despair, A Reappraisal of Spinoza's Philosophy* (1973); *Perceptual Assurance and the Reality of the World* (1974); and some 40 articles in many journals.

To these distinguished publications Phi Sigma Tau is pleased to add *The Problem of Evil.*

# THE PROBLEM OF EVIL

## I. The Problem for Theology

"The treatment of evil by theology," writes Brand Blanshard, "seems to me an intellectual disgrace."[1] My aim in this lecture is to ensure, so far as I am able, that the same indictment shall not be brought against philosophy. In so doing, I hope incidentally to show cause why, in the case of at least two outstanding theologians, it may not justly be brought against all theology, which at least has been aware of the problem virtually from its earliest beginnings.

Since biblical times the experience of evil has presented theists and theologians with what seems an insuperable obstacle to belief in the existence of a benevolent and all-powerful God. Unmerited misfortune and suffering, catastrophic disasters, and human malevolence have always seemed irreconcilable with an omnipotent creator of supreme justice and mercy. With this mystery Job and his admonitors wrestled; and their reasonings and protestations were finally silenced only by a declaration of the inscrutability of divine wisdom. But in that pronouncement the question is begged, for to accede to divine wisdom we must understand the principle of its justice, and what remains inscrutable to us we recognize neither as wise nor sensible. There must be some securer foundation for faith in the justice of the inscrutable than its unintelligibility.

In his progress to conversion St. Augustine encountered and overcame this hurdle; but his solution of the difficulty has proved less convincing to many than his statement of the problem:

Whence, then, is evil, since God who is good made all things good? It was the greater and supreme Good who made these lesser goods, but Creator and Creation are alike good. Whence then comes evil? . . . Could he who was omnipotent be unable to change matter wholly so that no evil might remain in it? Indeed why did He choose to make anything

of it and not rather by the same omnipotence cause it wholly not to be.[2]

St. Thomas Aquinas recognizes the same
objection to belief in God's existence:

It seems that God does not exist; because
if one of two contraries be infinite, the
other would be altogether destroyed.
But the name *God* means that he is infinite goodness. If therefore, God existed,
there would be no evil discoverable; but
there is evil in the world. Therefore God
does not exist.[3]

His reply to this objection is a reference to
Augustine, which still leaves the unbeliever
unconvinced, and the existence of evil has
remained the main bastion of the atheist's
case ever since. It has been reiterated by
Hume, John Stuart Mill, Bertrand Russell
and, more recently, by Antony Flew. And
now Professor Blanshard, perhaps the most
tolerant and urbane of critics, writes,

The question at issue is a straightforward one: how are the actual amount
and distribution of evil to be reconciled
with the government of the world by a
God who is in our sense good? So

straightforward a question deserves a straightforward answer, and it seems to me that only one such answer makes sense, namely that the two sides can *not* be reconciled.[4]

## II. The Problem for Philosophy

The question for the theist is thus succinctly stated, but summary denial of the existence of God does not dispose of the problem of evil. For God's existence is held to be incredible on rational principles, and reason demands a conception of the world which is coherent and self-consistent. The ground of the rejection of God's existence is its incompatibility with evils undeniably real, and these are the negation of values cherished by men and the frustrations of their best aspirations. But a world that engenders human beings who seek fulfillment in valued ends, yet implacably frustrates their desires is one which involves an irremediable conflict. Either human aspirations must be absurd and unnatural, and the values which they pursue and which give meaning to the term 'evil' must be irrational; in which case human valuations would be subverted without rendering the world coherent—for a world which spawns an irrational humanity cannot itself be rational. Or, if human aspirations are reasonable, it must be a perverse world that generates a race with inherent longing for a fulfillment impossible in the nature of things.

But, you may object, the world as we find it does permit us some limited satisfactions. Need we require more in order to pronounce it intelligible? The answer will be that we must if the argument is to stand which affirms the incompatibility of God with the existence of evil. For, unless the ultimate human aim were for more than some merely partial and qualified good, if it were not for a complete and total realization admitting of no residual regrets, the alleged ground for denying God's existence would be inadequate and his presumed benevolence would stand undefeated. For the presence of evil is not incompatible with partial realization of good, but only with total realization. We in our

impotence cannot achieve such total fulfillment, but unless we saw it as desirable,
we should not regard it as the necessary
aim of benevolent omnipotence. We are,
therefore, confronted with an ultimate
standard of value, in terms of which we
define evil as well as good, but one that is
inevitably rendered unrealizable by the
irremovable existence of evil. Were the
standard irrational the original dilemma
would be resolved, for then the evil identi-
fied by that standard would not be real.
But if the standard is what reason dictates,
the world with its irremediable evil is in-
coherent, positing an inevitable conflict
between its own character and the inherent
nature of its most developed product.

What reason demands of an omnipotent
deity, it cannot remit to an atheistic world.
If it is absurd to postulate a benevolent
God as creator and disposer of a vitiated
world, that same world without God, cul-
minating in an aspiring human nature that
finds evil irremediable, is no less absurd.
The problem of evil, therefore, is not confined to theology but is a metaphysical

problem that is not mitigated by denying God's existence, and is one that no philosopher can escape.

We might try to resolve the difficulty by following the lead of Professor Blanshard's theory and confining good and evil wholly to human concerns. Blanshard finds no element of value in the world apart from man. Nature at large is, for him, indifferent to value and in itself neutral. It is only with human consciousness that value comes into being, arising out of human impulse and desire. Evil should then be solely the object of man's aversion—what frustrates the rational desires of self-conscious persons. In Blanshard's words:

> The world appears to be a closely knit, intelligible order neutral to good and evil. Good and evil, so far as is known, are confined to one planet, and to one strand in the history of that planet, namely the evolution of striving minds. As regards value, the universe presents the appearance of a great plain stretching to the horizon on all sides, but exhibiting at one point an extraordinary

phenomenon—a tower that is being slow-
ly thrust upward into the sky. This is
the tower of purposive endeavor, . . . In
that solitary column, all values, so far
as we know, have had their precarious
career.[5]

In what sense a world such as this could
be an *intelligible* order is not clearly apparent. For in the unending featureless
plain depicted, how a conscious purposive
exception should emerge at all remains an
impenetrable enigma. And if it should
arise, generating beings vainly stretching
their yearning hands upward into the il-
limitable void, they surely must present a
totally ridiculous and futile spectacle.
What significance, even if it could be realized, would the self-fulfillment have of
so minute an excrescence in so vast a
wilderness?

It would have significance for itself,
Blanshard might answer. We need look no
further for its value, which is intrinsic and
self-satisfying. But we could grant that
only if the success of purposive endeavour
were at least a possibility, for if it were

not, the very urge of desire would be self-defeating; and on the account of the world we have been offered, the possibility of achievement seems more than doubtful. Apart from such doubts, however, we cannot isolate human endeavours from the world in which they are made, nor, despite Blanshard's insistence, can we regard the physical world as purely neutral and indifferent; and neither should he, for he has assured us that the universe is a closely knit order in which everything is causally and necessarily related to everything else.[6] Accordingly, not only must the evolution of living and intelligent beings on this planet have been conditioned throughout its course by effects coextensive with the physical world, and the nature of life and mind determined in every detail of its constitution by influences from its surrounding environment; but also in our efforts to attain our objectives we cannot be indifferent to the circumstances of the world in which we are set. As they are adverse or favorable we must value them. It is difficult to understand, therefore, in what sense the inanimate universe is neutral to our purposes. On the one hand, we and our aspiring nature are its products, and, on the other, it affords the conditions in which the success or failure of our projects is determined.

Moreover, the great mass of our experience tells us that these conditions are for the most part adverse to our aims, which are never wholly successful, but, on the contrary, always, in large measure, frustrated. The emergence of the striving nodule in the limitless expanse of unheeding desolation, therefore, must be wholly futile, and the total world-picture altogether bewildering and insane. For it offers us a blind mechanical system inexorably generating at one isolated point a race of conscious, desiring, striving beings, which it relentlessly and perpetually frustrates. The world so viewed involves a palpable contradiction, first in that the merely material and dead should somehow give rise to the self-conscious and aspiring; and, secondly, in that, having done so, it should negate and frustrate the aims of its own product.

Such a world, so far from being rational, is absurd—a good reason no doubt for denying the existence of God, but hardly a conclusion in which any sound philosophy can rest; for here we have *par excellence* the *reductio ad absurdum.* As I have said, human beings are inseparable from the encompassing world which surrounds and has produced them. They and their thinking are permeated by its matter, its influences and its properties. From an irrational world no rational creature can emerge by any intelligible process which does not violate the second law of thermodynamics. Chaos cannot naturally produce order. Accordingly, an absurd world can produce only absurd products and it should follow that the very thought of the man who philosophizes is itself absurd and philosophy would cancel itself out. No philosopher can consistently conclude by his own reasoning that he and his reasoning are insane—and none worthy of his salt could believe any such thing. It is indeed absurd to maintain that the world is absurd.

Belief in a rational universe without God yet one in which evil persists (the very reason for denying God's existence) is just as inconsistent as the belief in the existence of a benevolent God is said to be with the presence of evil. And if the presence of evil is taken to prove that the world is absurd, there would be no reason to reject even what was inconsistent. But that itself is an absurd and self-contradictory statement. On the other hand, if by any argument evil could be rendered intelligible in a rational world, it should in principle also be reconcilable with a God who is both omniscient (that is absolutely rational) and benevolent as well as omnipotent.

Professor Blanshard's doctrine, therefore, plunges us even more deeply into paradox than the theology which he castigates, for theology can at least consider the possibility that an omnipotent and supremely benevolent God may bring good out of evil, as St. Thomas, quoting Augustine, reminds us in his reply to the objection referred to above.[7] But that possibility has to be demonstrated and understood. To assert it baldly is no solution of the problem.

The aim of the philosopher is to make the universe and our experience of it intelligible to himself and others, and to that aim the existence of evil is as much an obstacle as it is to the theologian's belief in God. In fact, it becomes clear that the problem is really the same for both, when one realizes (with St. Augustine) that God and the ultimate standard of intelligibility are one and the same.[8]

## III. The Meaning of 'Evil'

Up to this point I have used the word 'evil' as a noun, as we commonly do in every-day parlance, as if evil were a kind of stuff to be encountered in the world like a metal, or more appropriately the dross rejected when the metal is refined. But the word 'evil' is more properly used as an adjective. It is an evaluative term indicating an attribute or quality of its subject. That things may have qualities apart from our awareness of them is commonly maintained, but this is not so obviously true of evaluative terms like good and bad; because for these terms to apply, their objects must be somehow satisfying or discomforting and therefore they involve a reference to human desire, or at least to animal impulse. In this regard Blanshard guides us in the right direction. Without human desire there is no evaluation, and of that human consciousness is the condition. Animal sentience and impulse certainly involve aversions and attractions, but these are only instinctive. It is we who judge them good or bad for the beast affected, by analogy with our own self-conscious experience.

Value, it seems, or at any rate evaluation, follows upon purpose, without which there is neither good nor bad, and we may concede to Blanshard that without human desire the terms would have no meaning. But human desire is more than blind appetite, for it involves awareness of its urge and anticipation of its object. And what is good is not simply what satisfies particular desires, for they conflict. Being aware of them and of ourselves, we are equally aware of the frustration occasioned by such conflict, and being rational we strive to remove it by ordering and evaluating the desires themselves and their ends. What is ultimately good is what satisfies the person as a whole and so we come to conclude that personality itself is the paramount value, agreeing with Plato that justice is a harmony in the soul and with Kant that humanity, in ourselves and others, is an end for its own sake. In all this we are still in agreement also with Blanshard, who maintains that good is human fulfillment and evil its frustration.

We must note, as well, that this fulfillment is conditional upon self-awareness and rationality. It follows upon our consciousness of our own desires and the compatibility of their satisfactions, and it depends upon our ability to organize our activities into a harmonious whole—that is to say, upon our rational capacity. We may conclude, then, that good is the realization and fulfillment in practice of our rational capacities through our self-conscious nature, and evil is whatever militates against such self-fulfillment. Moreover, as we have already noticed, to be completely satisfying the fulfillment must be total. We cannot be put off with half measures, but require for final acquiescence that which is the ultimate standard of evaluation, immaculate perfection.

In giving this brief explanation of the nature of evaluation, showing it to be inseparable from consciousness, desire and rationality, I have incidentally defined reason as the activity of ordering. To set in order is to organize and that again is to bring a multiplicity of elements into a unified whole, which is precisely the function of reason. It sets things in due order according to a principle of unity which constitutes a single system from diverse elements. To do this, however, more is required than simple aggregation. A heap of stones is a unity made up of a multiplicitiy, but it is hardly an organized system. The difference is that the heap is made up of the stones which are indifferent to it and to one another. They could all as well be what they are if heaped in some other way or scattered and apart; whereas in an organized system the parts are mutually adjusted, each modifies and is modified by all the rest, so that the nature of each part depends upon its place within the system and is dependent upon the plan, or organizing principle, of the whole. Nor is this irrelevant to purpose and evaluation, for we recognize a purpose as a design or plan. It is not simply the end-condition of a course of action, but an end that fulfills or completes a design, rounds off a pattern bringing some form of activity, or a complete life, into an ordered whole. As we said earlier, fulfillment is the satisfaction of the person as a harmonious whole. The end is thus the completion of a design, the realization of a 'rounded personality.'

There are, however, certain further features of systematic wholeness that I must list before proceeding. First, there can be no such whole without internal differentiations. An unarticulated unity may be a unit or singularity, but it is not a whole or system. Secondly, while the parts are mu-

tually adapted, and each determined by
the immanence in it of the principle of
order, no part, in as much as it is partial,
is an adequate realization of that principle.
To be partial is to be finite. Yet a series of
finites continuously being augmented *ad
infinitum* remains for ever incomplete and
is never whole. Thus it is endlessly finite.
Only what completes the whole can be
opposed to the partial. So in the last resort
the truly infinite must be self-complete,
and no progression to true infinity can be
endless. Such an infinite, however, exists
as such only in and through its articula-
tions, as they exist only in it and are constituted by its principle of order.

## IV.  The Wholeness of the Universe

Let us now reconsider the place of
value, as we have defined it, in the universe. We have agreed with Blanshard in
holding that value issues from the satisfaction of human desire and that fulfillment must be rational to be complete; but
we cannot accompany him in segregating

purposive conduct from the rest of the world.

First we must remember that purpose depends on consciousness, and intelligent action upon knowledge. Secondly, we must note that consciousness and knowledge are not the mere recording of the outside world in our awareness but the organization of our experience on systematic principles. If it were not so, our experience would be unintelligible and we should be incapable of scientific understanding. That we impose this order on the sensuously given was Kant's thesis. But if it had no connexion with or application to the world as it really is, our experience would be mere illusion and in no sense knowledge. Nor can this be the case, for we and our minds are parts of the real world. We are the products of nature; consequently our organizing activity must equally be its product, and lower nature from which we have sprung must be such as to produce us. This is true of life itself as well as conscious thought, which is its most developed activity, for life itself is organism—activities organized into a single self-maintaining system. It is a generally accepted law of physics that order cannot arise out of disorder within restricted bounds, and it is also the view of modern science that the physical universe is finite in extent, if self-contained and unbounded in form. Within this self-contained universe, therefore, it should follow that disorder cannot give rise to order and if the reality were merely chaos no life could ever emerge from it, nor any intelligent consciousness to impose order upon it. The emergence from physical nature of life and mind must therefore be rooted in some more elementary principle of order intrinsic to the physical world and there must be continuity throughout.

In that case the ultimate satisfaction of rational desire in human beings is at the same time the ultimate fulfillment of the evolutionary trend in the world as a whole, and we cannot, with Blanshard, regard any part of it as neutral or indifferent. Instead of a vast plain with a towering singularity at one point, a better simile would be a pyramid or cone of which the apex is continuous with the base and the summit supported and sustained by the mutually adjacent sections. But we shall find even this image unsatisfactory, because it reverses the logical order implied by the organizing principle the development of which we have declared to be continuous throughout.

## V. Dialectical System

The system as a whole, however, is not so simple as this outline of it suggests. It is not merely an evolutionary system but a dialectical totality, which is something far more complex. Taken on the purely physical level the world, as I have said, is a self-contained system. Within it all the physical laws and constants are (if we are to follow Sir Arthur Eddington) determined by its over-all structure. It is a whole of just the sort described above, in which all the parts and elements are mutually constituting and are determined by the universal principle of order. To exemplify this in detail (were I competent to do so) would take too long.[9] Let me mention only the identification by Einstein of matter with energy, the interdependence for relativity of time and space, velocity and distance, mass and motion. Eddington demonstrated mathematically that the number of particles in the universe was a function of the curvature of space and that the forces binding the components of the atom were determined by the radius of the universe. Everything in the universe, moreover, can be viewed and treated from the physical point of view as belonging to this system, living structures and processes no less than non-living.

Yet when we turn to life, the physical account, while still coextensive with its subject-matter, proves inadequate. It cannot encompass sentience and purpose. Attempts to show that it can, of which there are many, always surreptitiously assume a non-physical principle which remains latent and unacknowleged in the explanation given. Living organisms are more complexly integrated and behave more efficiently as self-maintaining systems than anything at the merely inorganic level. And, again, life can, or must, to be adequately understood, be regarded as a single world-wide biotic whole. No sharp line can be drawn between organism and environment.[10] Life exists only in eco-systems, the inter-relations of whose parts is throughout organic; so that, while for certain purposes, we may distinguish between lesser and greater, more exclusive and more inclusive, strictly they are all interdependent and can be confined within no limits short of the whole universe, viewed as a single biocoenosis.

Finally, on the basis of sentience arise consciousness and intellect issuing in knowledge, which, distributed though it is among a myriad subjects, ideally constitutes a single system.[11] Within this system the accounts we give of the world as a physical and as a biotic whole are contained, and without it those spheres exist as ordered wholes only implicitly. A system of the kind I am trying to describe implies the immanence in all of its parts of the whole which they articulate. To be itself each part must register and reflect, by adjustment to all the others, the systematic structure. But short of consciousness, in

which this relationship is not only explicit but necessary, it is masked by a sur-
face appearance of independence between
things. Consciousness, however, is possible
only for a unitary subject for whom inter-
relations have become apparent and the
interplay of their terms is made evident. It
is only for developed consciousness that
the systematic nature of the universe at
any and every level is explicit—only for the
scientist and the philosopher. In themselves, the biological and physical structures are expressed in mutual reactivity of
their parts, but are elaborated and coher-
ently apprehended as wholes only when
brought to consciousness.

For this reason, the explanation and intelligibility of the lower levels—their true
nature—is to be discovered only in the
higher. It is only what finally emerges that
can properly account for the rudimentary
beginnings; and what has been called
the Noosphere[12]—the totality of cognitive
awareness—alone actualizes and fully realizes what exists potentially in the prior
phases of the scale. Each of these self-

complete and self-contained wholes is continuous with, and in some sense presupposes, its predecessor. Yet each successive whole realizes more adequately what its predecessor cannot encompass. They form a continuous scale although each is, on its own terms, self-sufficient. And though they are continuous they are also mutually in contrast—inanimate to animate, material to ideal. Finally, among the internal details of each, a similar structure, if we had time and opportunity to investigate it, would be revealed.[13] Because the scale is continuous the entire gamut constitutes a single whole, and because the highest stage incorporates all the lower ones, it is not only the consummation but also in itself the totality.

This is the nature of a dialectical whole, and once again it must be stressed that it is a whole only in and through its articulation into the parts and elements which constitute it, while they are what they are only in virtue of the universal principle of order. But that principle is not fully realized short of the complete totality.

You must not be misled, by the brevity

of my description, into thinking that the
system is a static pattern, for it is just the
contrary. I have set out only the general
framework. At every level and in every
phase it is dynamic, an activity or process.
At the physical level every phase is an
energy system; according to Erwin Schröd-
inger's description, a flux on which a
*Gestalt* or configuration is imposed defin-
ing its physical manifestation.[14] At the biological level every organic whole is an
open system constantly exchanging matter
and energy with its surroundings. And at
the psychological level every experience is
an activity of ordering and relating elements in feeling and consciousness.

The driving force of this process throughout is the inadequacy of the part to the
whole that is immanent in it. Physical systems are constantly toppling and reassert-
ing their equilibria in response to more
inclusive tensions within a wider sphere.
In organic open systems the equilibrium is
continuously breaking down and perpetually being reconstituted and augmented. In
consciousness the apparent shortcomings—

the problematic nature—of the object is what constantly impels the mind to new syntheses.[15] Finiteness is the character of every partial element, or lower phase in the scale; and because the part, or phase, is determined by the principle of the total order which is immanent in it, its inadequacy to the whole sets it in opposition to what it lacks and omits, and impels it to coalesce with or adjust itself to its opposite, to constitute a more adequate structure. The dynamic force of progression is thus the contradiction set up in all finite forms by their inadequacy to the totality immanent in them. To give but one example— especially relevant to our problem—human desire is a feeling of want and inadequacy, which sets up a tension between the present condition of the subject and the completion or fulfillment envisaged, so that it becomes the motivation of action seeking a satisfaction that is, as I said earlier, the completion of a design.

Human life and consciousness, however, while obviously a very late and highly developed stage in the scale, are as obviously

not its final culmination. Human personality while constantly striving for self-fulfillment cannot attain it within its own
limits. In the first place, no individual person is or can be self-sufficient either intellectually or practically. Secondly, complete
fulfillment must be at once aesthetic, intellectual and moral, and that would require
the complete rationalization and sublimation of natural impulse. Thirdly, such fulfillment involves a self-identification of the
finite individual with the infinite totality
in which he consciously finds himself to be
a member. It thus requires a self-tran-
scendence of the finite through an atone-
ment with and absorption into a higher
form of being than the simply temporal,
the merely ephemeral and transitory.

We can now recognize the unsuitability
of our former image as a representation of
the structure of the universe. A pyramid or
cone is, in the first place, too static; but a
second and even more serious fault is that
it suggests the priority of the lower levels
to the higher and represents the culmination as a more restricted reality than the

base. A cylinder might have been better but still far from satisfactory, because the upper layers are not simply supported by the lower but actualize the potentialities of the latter and are in some sense their *raison d'être*. The system is more like a developing organism, a continuous movement or process of change in which the phases are determined by the structure of what is finally to emerge, and the *nisus* is the tension between the rudimentary nature of the initial germplasm and the mature form of the developed organism.

## VI.   The Nature and Place of Evil

It is time to return to St. Augustine's question, 'Whence is evil?' I said above that evil was what prevented or frustrated human rational fulfillment and now I can extend this definition somewhat. Human nature and activity, we saw, are not separable from the universe in which they occur, and the brief account I have given of that universe represents it as a dialectical scale of forms ranging from electromagnetic waves, through atoms and molecules to organisms and intelligent human beings. Human purpose, therefore, is but the manifestation at a highly developed level of a universal principle of ordering immanent throughout the world, and realizing itself fully only in the totality. Moreover, human personality is itself a totality the fulfillment of which involves a combination of intellectual, moral and artistic excellence as well as the realization of other potentialities. These excellences are each and all of them the articulation in systematic detail of universal principles of the same general character as that we have been examining. This is, perhaps, most obviously exemplified in the intellectual aspect, for science is systematic knowledge developed systematically into a unified whole. Moreover, the process of perfecting these capacities is dialectical[16] in the manner already described. What hinders and frustrates this process is evil. It is what obstructs the development and restricts the subject to a lower phase, holding it down to a more finite level. If we extend our definition to this formula we can apply it to every level of the cosmic scale, although its application below the human will be proleptic, because, prior to human consciousness, it is not recognized and so is not evaluated.

In this wider meaning it is apparent that evil is incident upon finiteness, the characteristic of the partial and inadequate, or, as we naturally say, it is defect. Let me exemplify briefly. At the organic level whatever disrupts or truncates the organismic system is disease or harm to the organism—that is, evil. But organisms are subject to such harm only insofar as they are finite and so fail completely to maintain their systematic wholeness in relation to their environment. Intellectual evil is error, stupidity, or ignorance—obvious functions of limitation and finiteness. Moral evil is the failure to order and rationalize our natural impulses, again an incident of finitude, consequent upon restriction to a lower grade in nature than our rational capacity implies. In all cases, evil is restriction, the badge and insignia of the finite.

It is not, therefore, anything substantial,

but is merely the negative aspect of what in its positive being is good. To revert to our examples, disease is the positive re-action of the organism to the effect of an-other positive influence (on the part of viruses or bacteria, or the like) which tends to disrupt the organic self-maintenance of its system. Each positive trend is construc-tive and self-maintaining but they come into conflict. The evil involved is simply the degree to which the superior and more inclusive system fails to preserve its in-tegrity. Evil is no positive entity or process. Similarly, stupidity is failure of insight and confusion of constructive thinking. So far as it is an effort to think and understand it is positive and good; and if it were not these at all it could not become confused nor would there be any attempt to com-prehend which could fail. Lastly, if we did not constantly strive to satisfy our de-sires, did not seek contentment and per-sonal fulfillment, the material of moral action would be altogether lacking and so equally the means and occasion of moral failure. Wickedness is neither more nor

less than the persistent effort to fulfill one-
self in ways which negate the very conditions of fulfillment both of ourselves and of
others. Its positive content and aspect is its
tendency to and potentiality of good, but
through confusion of thought, or dispro-
portionate passion in the agent (again the
incidents of finitude) the tendency is di-
verted from its proper course and the
potency is frustrated.

But here we must anticipate what may
become a veritable chorus of objections.
First, it will be protested, mere limitation
is not necessarily evil. The beauty of a
snowflake is not marred by its smallness.
The excellence of a novel is not increased
with its length. And the capacity of an animal to survive is actually reduced by in-
creasing its size beyond certain propor-
tions. But this objection answers itself by
implication. The limitations of such things
are not infringements but actually en-
hancements of their structural wholeness.
The symmetry and pattern of the snowflake are internally perfect; the artistic
merit of a novel, or of any work of art, de-

pends not on its size or prolongation, but on its structure and inner coherence; and the adaptability of an organism depends on the adjustment of its organs in shape and size to the functions they must perform to maintain its organic integrity. This sort of limitation—determination by a structural principle—is the opposite of evil. What ranks as disvalue is the kind of limitation which prevents such a principle from actualizing its potentialities: the limitation of the snowflake to certain ranges of temperature, beyond which it inevitably disintegrates; the limitation of the work of art to a medium or to a sensuous form, so that its aesthetic content and meaning can be conveyed only by indirection or symbolically; the limitation of an organism to certain chemicophysical cycles which necessarily involve vulnerability, eventual degeneration and death. It is this sort of limitation to which evil is concomitant.

A more serious objection would be that evil is surely something over and above mere finiteness. It has a positive reality that cannot be reduced to mere privation.

Suffering which is neither merited nor functional, even if consequent upon finiteness, has an intrinsic badness whatever its cause. And what of human malevolence? It is hardly a necessary consequence of limited capacity, but rather increases in reprehensibility with the physical prowess and intellectual competence of the perpetrator.

This is indeed the case and the abhorrence of evil cannot be argued away, nor is it mitigated or denied by the allegation that it is an incident of finiteness. Yet it is no less true that liability to suffering is conditioned by the limitations within which living things can maintain their integrity, and that pain, which is beneficent as a warning signal against harm, becomes exaggerated beyond this functional utility only because of the organism's restriction to limited remedial reactions. Moral turpitude is not simply correlative to lack of natural capacity and need not accompany every such limitation. But wherever it does occur, it is due to a finiteness that turns awry potentially wholesome tendencies, or an obtuseness which cannot comprehend certain evaluative implications, or an emotional violence which stems from obscurer instinctive sources resistant to higher regulation and control. All human immorality is the expression of urges and drives to fulfill desires that aim at self-satisfaction, but seek it, due to some limitation or obfuscation of insight, in objects inadequate to that aim. The conclusion, therefore, remains valid that evil is the incident of finiteness.

Finitude, however, is partiality or inadequacy to the whole. It is what constitutes a mere factor, or moment, or lower phase of the dialectical scale. And the dialectical scale is the self-differentiation of the principle of wholeness which realizes itself fully in the ultimate consummation, which is at the same time the whole system. To this consummation every part, every moment, and every phase is indispensable, for each is one expression of the principle of structure which constitutes the whole—the principle that is immanent in every element but also transcendent beyond all finite manifestations.

All the forms and degrees of finitude, therefore, are essential and indispensable to the being and realization of the ultimate perfection. For it realizes itself through them and realizes their potentialities in itself. And evil, as the incident of finitude, is precisely what is being progressively overcome in the course of that realization. It is both necessary to it and is transformed by it.

The utimate perfection moreover, what is both transcendent beyond and immanent in the finite, is what the theist recognizes as God. It is Plato's Idea of the Good, the ultimate object of all desire, which is beyond being and knowing, yet creates and sustains all things, makes everything intelligible and the mind intelligent. It is Augustine's Truth: the Wisdom that transcends the human intellect and is the goal of all desire as the condition of happiness. It is that, for Anselm, than which a greater is inconceivable. It is the Substance of Spinoza and the Absolute Spirit of Hegel.

And because it is the transcendent consummation of a dialectical system which is
integral to its nature, and in every element
and phase of which it is immanent, the
finite is essential to its self-specification,
yet is continuously reconstituted into fuller
adequacy to, and harmony with, the whole.
Evil, therefore, while intrinsic to its
process, is nevertheless progressively elim-
inated in its becoming, and is wholly an-
nulled in its realization.

It follows that evil is an actuality. It
exists and is, in an important sense, real;
but only as an incident of finitude. It is
only the finite that experiences evil, and
to the extent that the finite is transcended,
evil evaporates and vanishes. Pain is evil
only to those whose power of mind,
whether through psychological, moral, or
religious elevation, cannot overcome it—
that is, to the finite. That such mental elevation can overcome it there is ample evidence in hypnosis, yoga, the heroism of
martyrs, and the experience of mystics.
Even so mundane a capacity as understanding overcomes pain, for suffering is

in large measure emotional and emotion is transformed by the rational comprehension of its cause. Consider how one's anger toward an insult abates when one realizes that it was the result of a misapprehension. Similarly fear generated by pain subsides when one understands either that it is remedial, or alternatively irremediable.

But pain is not in itself evil, only in its deleterious effects upon moral character. Intrinsic evil is moral dereliction which is evil primarily for the agent—as Socrates and the Stoics maintained. Yet, as I have argued, every *propensity* and impulse is in itself good and becomes bad only by misdirection. Its intrinsic tendency is towards good, and its failure when it goes astray is the stimulus to its reformation. The nisus which drives the finite, even in its shortcoming and degradation, is that toward the elimination of evil, once it is supplemented by what it lacks. Its movement is always dialectical, and the structure of the dialectical whole which is immanent in it is the progressive transfiguration of the finite.

## VII.  Solution of the Problem

Unless the whole is articulated, in infinite diversification, however, it cannot be
a concrete totality. It cannot be merely
transcendent and still be concretely real.
Such a conception of God would typically
be a metaphysical abstraction, the much
berated God of the philosophers. The true
and living God must be both immanent
and transcendent, both infinitely self-dif-
ferentiated and wholly self-complete. The
infinite beyond the finite is another finite
and a mere idea, but the concrete infinite
is that which is realized in and through the
finite which is its own self-differentiation.
In the language of religion, God expresses
his infinity in his creation—'the heavens
declare the glory of God.' Only in and
through articulation is there an infinite
whole; only in and through articulation is
there anything finite, and only as an incident of finitude is there any evil. Evil is
thus a transient but inevitable characteristic of the self-differentiation of a perfection which annuls and transfigures the

finite in realizing its potencies and fulfill-
ing its aspirations, which are after all nothing other than the immanence in the finite
of the transcendent infinite. And it is precisely this perpetual overcoming of evil in
the course of which it is itself the goad and
stimulus to reformation and advance, this
progressive transfiguration of the finite by
absorption into his own perfection, which
consitutes the transcendent beneficence of
God.

The omnipotence of God, meanwhile, is
what Spinoza called the power of existing.
It is that energy or activity by which anything exists that does exist. It is that nisus
by which anything progresses, or grows, or
evolves. It is the immanence in all finite
beings of the infinity which they diversify.
But diversification implies specificity and
particularity, or finiteness. Without it there
could be no concrete whole, which, as a
whole, is constituted by its self-differentia-
tions and is the outcome of their process.
Finiteness, or specificity, at the same time
involves defect and thus is the breeding
ground of evil. There can be no escape

from this implication of evil in finitude, nor of finitude in the articulation of the infinite. For God to have created a world devoid of evil would have been for him not to create a world at all; and a God that does not create is an inactive God, an abstraction—in short, not God at all.

The idea of a world without evil, is the idea of a world without differentiation and finiteness. It is, in short, a self-contradiction and an absurdity, and to create an absurdity is not a mark of omniscience, nor is it a limitation of power to be unable to produce a self-contradiction. That God creates a world is thus the exercise of his omnipotence and that it contains evil is the concomitant product of that omnipotence. The contradiction lies in the presumption that it could be otherwise, not in the fact that it is so. At the same time, God's power is that nisus which impels the finite towards transcendence of itself and realization of its potentialities issuing in an infinitude that coincides with God's divine nature. In the perpetual overcoming of evil the power and goodness of God coincide and the compatibility of evil with absolute infinity is finally demonstrated.[17]

## VIII.  Vindication of Augustine and Aquinas

The solution of the problem I have offered is wholly in accord with the teachings of Augustine and Aquinas, even though the statements of their position differ in form. St. Augustine understands by God a being who is absolutely good, the source of all being and all goodness; the truth or ultimate wisdom, the possession of which is the condition of happiness and is the goal and motive of all desire.[18] As such the power of God is immanent in all things and is the motivating force at least of human action.

Augustine infers, from the assumption that God is perfectly good and that he is the source and creator of everything, that everything so created is good, because being is *ipso facto* good, as it is the product of the supreme being, which is wholly good.[19] But there are degrees of being and

goodness. Some being is incorruptible and
some corruptible. The incorruptible is the
infinite and eternal; the corruptible is the
finite. But to be corruptible it must be
good in the first instance and its corruption
is simply the privation of that good.[20] Evil,
therefore, is not a substance, but is merely
the privation of good.[21] In short, evil is the
incident of finiteness, and that again is
a matter of degree, in a world which
traverses all degrees of perfection. For
God has created a whole in which diverse things are harmonized and mutually
adapted.[22] Accordingly, evil is corruption
of the good, and in man's case corruption
of the will. But the will is corruptible because it is free and being free it is a great
good, without which there could be no
virtue, nor achievement, nor faith. Its cor-
ruptibility, again, is due to the finiteness
or insufficiency of man, whose will is inadequate to ultimate achievement and requires besides the grace and mercy of
God.[23] Accordingly, the cure of evil is not
its dismissal into some other place, for it
is nothing in itself—no substance—but is

the restoration of what is lacking to the sufferer (or perpetrator, as the case may be). In other words, it is the realization of the potentialities of the finite. And God, being good, would not permit such corruption unless by his consummate power he could bring good out of evil.[24]

If one interprets all this in terms of the immanence of the infinite in the finite, and of the finite as the self-specification of the infinite, we have virtually the same doctrine as I have been at pains to expound.

For Augustine, it is the power of God working in and through the finite and corrupt that brings good out of evil, a process of which the entire progression described in the *Confessions* is an example. The dialectical account of the matter which I have tried to set out makes his position entirely acceptable and intelligible. That Augustine's conception of the order of things is implicitly dialectical is clear from his statements in *De Libero Arbitrio*. Not only does he divide goods into grades and point out that the evil of the higher grade (e.g. sin) is better than the good of lower grades (e.g. physical light), but he also argues that suffering is part of the perfection of the created order, because "the order of creation from the highest to the lowest occurs by just degrees."[25] The implication is clear that unless there were lower orders the whole would not be perfect, which is what we have maintained above.

In the *Summa Theologica* of Aquinas this position is more explicit and direct. That evil is not a substance or a 'nature' is the first point Thomas establishes. It is mere privation of good, and in itself is neither being nor good.[26] It is a privation and not a simple negation, as we have already observed. The limitation of a thing which is dictated by its special form, its peculiar wholeness or specific nature, is not evil, only the deprivation of what wholeness or perfection requires. But Aquinas' second point is the most fundamental. The distinction of things in the universe and their multitude, he says are produced by God in order that his goodness might be communicated to and represented by creatures. To this end a multi-

plicity is necessary so that what is want-
ing in one might be supplied by another.
Hence the whole universe together par-
ticipates the divine goodness more perfectly than any one creature alone.[27] Similarly, the inequality of things, as well as
their multiplicity is necessary to the divine
goodness and wisdom. "For the universe
would not be perfect if only one grade
of goodness were found in things."[28] So,
with respect to evil Aquinas can go on to
say:

The perfection of the universe requires
that there should be inequality in things,
so that every grade of goodness may be
realized. Now, one grade of goodness is
that of the good which cannot fail. Another grade of goodness is that of the
good which can fail in goodness. These
grades of goodness are to be found in
being itself; for there are some things
which cannot lose their being, as incorruptible things, while there are some
which can lose their being, as corruptible things. As, therefore, the perfection
of the universe requires that there

should be not only incorruptible beings,
but also corruptible beings, the perfection of the universe requires that there
should be some which can fail in goodness and which sometimes do fail. Now
it is in this that evil consists . . .²⁹

In this way God is the cause of evil, insofar as he acts with a view to the perfection of the universe as a whole, but is not
the cause of evil, insofar as he creates only
being which is good, and yet becomes subject to evil by privation. That, however, is
neither good nor being and so is not di-
rectly God's creation. Neither is it created
by any other principle; for privation is privation of form which is the principle of
goodness—that for the sake of which everything exists and to attain which everything
strives. And form is the actualization of the
potential. So the subject of form which
is the potential is equally the subject of
privation. The potential, however, is matter which is the potency of becoming informed (and so of realizing the good).
Accordingly, every actual being, *qua* actual
(or informed) is so far good and every

potential being is potentially good.[30] Evil, in consequence, is incident upon finitude, matter or the privation of form, which is itself the potentiality of good.

Aquinas is using different terminology from that which I have adopted. His is mainly Aristotelian, and Aristotle's system is essentially dialectical like the one I have tried to outline. If then, this is indeed the typical structure of the universe, a solution to the problem of evil is possible both for philosophy and for theology, and its treatment so far as it follows lines similar to those laid down by Augustine and Aquinas, is hardly as intellectually bankrupt as Professor Blanshard has alleged.

## NOTES

1. *Reason and Belief* (New Haven: Yale University Press, 1975), p. 546.

2. *Confessions*, Book VII, v. (F. J. Sheed translation).

3. *Summa Theologica*, I, q. 2, a. 3, obj. 1 (English Dominican translation).

4. *Reason and Belief*, loc. cit.

5. *Ibid.*, p. 538.

6. *Ibid.*, Ch. XIII.

7. Aquinas, *Summa Theologica*, I, q. 2, a. 3, ad. 1; Augustine, *Enchiridion*, XI.

8. *Confessions*, Book III, v; Book V, iii; Book VII, x; Book X, xxiii, xxiv; *De Libero Arbitrio*, Book II, xv.

9. See, however, my discussion in *The Foundations of Metaphysics in Science* (London: Allen and Unwin, 1965), Chs. II-VII; also D. W. Sciama, *The Unity of the Universe* (New York: Doubleday, 1959) and Sir Arthur Eddington, *The Expanding Universe* (Cambridge University Press, 1933), *New Pathways in Science* (Cambridge University Press, 1935), *The Philosophy of Physical Science* (Cambridge University Press, 1939).

10. Cf. J. S. Haldane, *Organism and Environment* (New Haven: Yale University Press, 1917).

11. Cf. Pierre Teilhard de Chardin, *The Phenomenon of Man*, trans. Bernard Wall (New York: Harper and Brothers, 1959), Book Three.

12. Cf. Theilhard, *loc. cit.*

13. Briefly, in the physical sphere we have the series: energy waves, wavepackets or particles, atoms,

THE PROBLEM OF EVIL

molecules, crystals (periodic and aperiodic). In the biological sphere we have macromolecules, viruses, bacteria, cells, unicellular organisms, colonial organisms, multicellular organisms and the whole range of plants and animals. In the sphere of mind we have sentience, feeling, perception, imagination, intellect and rational knowledge. Cf. my *The Foundations of Metaphysics in Science* (see note 9 above) and *Hypothesis and Perception* (London: Allen and Unwin, 1970) where some attempt to work out the system in more detail is made.

14. Cf. *What Is Life? and Other Scientific Essays* (Garden City: Doubleday Anchor, 1956).

15. The detailed evidence for all this is too massive to summarize here. Cf. my *Hypothesis and Perception*, Ch. VIII, and *Perceptual Assurance and the Reality of The World* (Worcester: Clark University Press, 1974); also J. Piaget, *La Psychologie de l'Intelligence* (Paris: Cohn, 1947; trans. Piercy and Bertyne, New York: Harcourt Brace, 1950).

16. *Hypothesis and Perception*, Chs. VI, XI, XII.

17. The objection may well be made that pain and evil prior to their overcoming and transformation into good are positively bad and that nothing I have said removes that badness. But this is to overlook the unity of the totality. The whole, while it is differentiated and generates itself through finite phases, is nevertheless a single system in which the ultimate realization does not exist apart from its precedent phases. It is at once all of them (immanent in them) and their fulfillment—the actualization of their potentialities (transcendent to them). The transfiguration

of the finite is thus in very truth the sublimation of all evil which the eyes of God are too pure to behold (Habbakuk, I, 13).

18. Cf. *De Libero Arbitrio*, Book I, ix-xv.
19. *Confessions*, Book VII, xii, xv; *Enchiridion*, XII, XIII.
20. *Ibid.*, Book VII, xi-xii.
21. *Ibid.*, Book VII, xvi; *Enchiridion*, XI, XII.
22. *Confessions*, Book VII, xv.
23. *Enchiridion*, XXXII. Cf. *De Libero Arbitrio*, Book II, xviii-xx.
24. *Enchiridion*, XI, quoted by Aquinas in *Summa Theologica*, I, q. 2, a. 3.
25. *Op. cit.* Book III, ix. Cf. also xi.
26. *Summa Theologica,* I, q. 48, a. 1.
27. *Ibid.,* I, q. 47, a. 1.
28. *Ibid.,* I, q. 47, a. 2.
29. *Ibid.,* I, q. 48, a. 2.
30. *Ibid.,* I, q. 48, a. 3.

# The Aquinas Lectures

Published by the Marquette University Press
Milwaukee, Wisconsin 53233

❧

*Humanism and Theology* (1943) by **Werner** Jaeger, Ph.D., Litt.D., (1888-1961) University professor, Harvard University. <small>SBN</small> 87462-107-0

*The Nature and Origins of Scientism* (1944) by John Wellmuth. <small>SBN</small> 87462-108-9

*Cicero in the Courtroom of St. Thomas Aquinas* (1945) by E. K. Rand, Ph.D., Litt.D., LL.D., (1871-1945) Pope professor of Latin, *emeritus,* Harvard University. <small>SBN</small> 87462-109-7

*St. Thomas and Epistemology* (1946) by Louis-Marie Regis, O.P., Th.L., Ph.D., director of the Albert the Great Institute of Mediaeval Studies, University of Montreal.

<small>SBN</small> 87462-110-0

*St. Thomas and the Greek Moralists* (1947, Spring) by Vernon J. Bourke, Ph.D., professor of philosophy, St. Louis University, St. Louis, Missouri. <small>SBN</small> 87462-111-9

*History of Philosophy and Philosophical Education* (1947, Fall) by Etienne Gilson of the *Académie française,* director of studies and professor of the history of Mediaeval philosophy, Pontifical Institute of Mediaeval Studies, Toronto. <small>SBN</small> 87462-112-7

*The Natural Desire for God* (1948) by William R. O'Connor, S.T.I Ph.D., former professor of dogmatic theology, St. Joseph's Seminary, Dunwoodie, N.Y. <small>SBN</small> 87462-113-5

*St. Thomas and the World State* (1949) by Robert M. Hutchins, former Chancellor of the University of Chicago, president of the Fund for the Republic.  SBN 87462-114-3

*Method in Metaphysics* (1950) by Robert J. Henle, S.J., Ph.D., academic vice-president, St. Louis University, St. Louis, Missouri.
SBN 87462-115-1

*Wisdom and Love in St. Thomas Aquinas* (1951) by Étienne Gilson of the *Académie française,* director of studies and professor of the history of Mediaeval philosophy, Pontifical Institute of Mediaeval Studies, Toronto.
SBN 87462-116-X

*The Good in Existential Metaphysics* (1952) by Elizabeth G. Salmon, Ph.D., professor of philosophy in the graduate school, Fordham University.  SBN 87462-117-8

*St. Thomas and the Object of Geometry* (1953) by Vincent Edward Smith, Ph.D., director, Philosophy of Science Institute, St. John's University.  SBN 87462-118-6

*Realism and Nominalism Revisited* (1954) by Henry Veatch, Ph.D., professor and chairman of the department of philosophy, Northwestern University.  SBN 87462-119-4

*Imprudence in St. Thomas Aquinas* (1955) by Charles J. O'Neil, Ph.D., professor of philosophy, Villanova University.  SBN 87462-120-8

*The Truth That Frees* (1956) by Gerard Smith, S.J., Ph.D., professor of philosophy, Marquette University. sBN 87462-121-6

*St. Thomas and the Future of Metaphysics* (1957) by Joseph Owens, C.Ss.R., Ph.D., professor of philosophy, Pontifical Institute of Mediaeval Studies, Toronto. sBN 87462-122-4

*Thomas and the Physics of 1958: A Confrontation* (1958) by Henry Margenau, Ph.D., Eugene Higgins professor of physics and natural philosophy, Yale University. sBN 87462-123-2

*Metaphysics and Ideology* (1959) by Wm. Oliver Martin, Ph.D., professor of philosophy, University of Rhode Island. sBN 87462-124-0

*Language, Truth and Poetry* (1960) by Victor M. Hamm, Ph.D., professor of English, Marquette University. sBN 87462-125-9

*Metaphysics and Historicity* (1961) by Emil L. Fackenheim, Ph.D., professor of philosophy, University of Toronto. sBN 87462-126-7

*The Lure of Wisdom* (1962) by James D. Collins, Ph.D., professor of philosophy, St. Louis University. sBN 87462-127-5

*Religion and Art* (1963) by Paul Weiss, Ph.D. Sterling professor of philosophy, Yale University. sBN 87462-128-3

*St. Thomas and Philosophy* (1964) by Anton C. Pegis, Ph.D., professor of philosophy, Pontifical Institute of Mediaeval Studies, Toronto.
SBN 87462-129-1

*The University In Process* (1965) by John O. Riedl, Ph.D., dean of faculty, Queensboro Community College.
SBN 87462-130-5

*The Pragmatic Meaning of God* (1966) by Robert O. Johann, associate professor of philosophy, Fordham University.

SBN 87462-131-3

*Religion and Empiricism* (1967) by John E. Smith, Ph.D., professor of philosophy, Yale University.
SBN 87462-132-1

*The Subject* (1968) by Bernard Lonergan, S.J., S.T.D., professor of Dogmatic Theory, Regis College, Ontario and Gregorian University, Rome.
SBN 87462-133-X

*Beyond Trinity* (1969) by Bernard J. Cooke, S.T.D.
SBN 87462-134-8

*Ideas and Concepts* (1970) by Julius R. Weinberg, Ph.D., (1908-1971) Vilas Professor of Philosophy, University of Wisconsin.
SBN 87462-135-6

*Reason and Faith Revisited* (1971) by Francis H. Parker, Ph.D., head of the philosophy department, Purdue University, Lafayette, Indiana.
SBN 87462-136-4

*Psyche and Cerebrum* (1972) by John N. Findlay, M.A. Oxon., Ph.D., Clark Professor of Moral Philosophy and Metaphysics, Yale University.
ISBN 0-87462-137-2

*The Problem of the Criterion* (1973) by Roderick M. Chisholm, Ph.D., Andrew W. Mellon Professor in the Humanities, Brown University.
ISBN 0-87462-138-0

*Man as Infinite Spirit* (1974) by James H. Robb, Ph.D., professor of philosophy, Marquette University.
ISBN 0-87462-139-9

*The Beginning and the Beyond* (1975) by Eric Voegelin, Ph.D. In preparation.

*Aquinas to Whitehead: Seven Centuries of Metaphysics of Religion* (1976) by Charles E. Hartshorne, Ph.D., professor of philosophy, the University of Texas at Austin.
ISBN 0-87462-141-0

*The Problem of Evil* (1977) by Errol E. Harris, D.Litt., Distinguished Visiting Professor of Philosophy, Marquette University.
ISBN 0-87462-142-8

Uniform format, cover and binding.